20/20 VISION

20/20 VISION

How Exodus 20:20 Brings the Purpose of Our Trials Into Focus

Sara B. Anderson, J.D.

Copyright © 2020 by **Sara B. Anderson, J.D.**

All rights reserved. No part of this publication may be reproduced, distributed or transmitted in any form or by any means, electronic or mechanical, including photocopying, recording, informational storage or retrieval systems, without prior written permission by the publisher or the author, except where permitted by law, for the purpose of review, or where otherwise noted.

BNA Publishing
P.O. Box 90453
Austin, TX 78709

Publisher's Note: Locales and public names are sometimes used for atmospheric purposes. Examples cited are composites based on the author's experience, not on any particular situation with a person or couple. Any resemblance to actual people, living or dead, or to businesses, companies, events, institutions, or locales is completely coincidental. This book does not replace or substitute for professional advice or services. Any information received from this book is not intended to be used in diagnosis, treatment, or as a cure. This book is sold with the understanding that neither the author nor the publisher is engaged through this book in rendering professional advice or services.

20/20 Vision: How Exodos 20:20 / Sara B. Anderson. -- 1st ed.
ISBN 978-0-5786410-5-8 Paperback
ISBN 978-0-5786412-0-1 Ebook

Unless otherwise indicated, Scripture quotations are from The Holy Bible, English Standard Version® (ESV®), copyright © 2001 by Crossway, a publishing ministry of Good News Publishers. Used by permission. All rights reserved.

CONTENTS

Chapter 1   Looking Back to Look Forward......................1
Chapter 2   My Life Was Normal Until. 7
Chapter 3   Through the Looking Glass 19
Chapter 4   Bringing the Desert into Focus 31
Chapter 5   Insight on the Mountaintop........................43
Chapter 6   Mountaintop Reconciliation.......................55
Chapter 7   Hope in the Desert......................................67

Worksheet I - Your Desert Experience/s 71
Worksheet II - Encountering God and His Wisdom........77
About the Author 83

Dedication to My Children

To know God's love transcends any circumstances of this life

"*Do not fear, for God has come to test you, that the fear of him may be before you, that you may not sin*"

—MOSES TO THE PEOPLE OF ISRAEL

CHAPTER ONE

Looking Back to Look Forward

What does Exodus 20:20 have to say to us in the 2020s? A lot as it turns out. When the calendar turned over to 2020 many of us welcomed the new decade with cautious optimism. The tumultuous 2010's put us through some tough times individually, nationally, and globally. We are left wondering—*hoping*—that the 2020s will usher in a new era of peace and prosperity.

As a whole, society is at a tipping point. We have no united standard for economic, social, or moral issues. Everyone is left to define his or her own standards, without regard for a consistent and unwavering anchor of truth. In the name of freedom, society has built an ideology from an unstable benchmark of relativism, resulting in confusion and unrest rather than security and hope.

Without a transcendent and perfect standard from which to gauge our beliefs, we have no consistent method to measure right and wrong. We are left reeling from insecurity as we ask, On which side of the line will my beliefs and actions fall? Many of us won't wait for the answer. Instead, we will resort to dropping our beliefs altogether. But, as the saying goes, If you stand for nothing, you will fall for anything. Alas, nothing of significance has been added to our united quest for truth.

So instead of offering us stability, subjective truth has left us floundering for footing. It offers little explanation for the problems we experience and little hope of finding a real solution. Desperate, we grasp for something in which we can place our hope. If we can't solve our problems on our own, then hopefully someone or something else can.

But in the quest to "go along to get along," most of us won't look to our parents' religion to solve our problems.

Post-modern thought insists that religion has failed to serve its purpose and that historical lessons are no longer relevant. Instead, human intellect is seen as the source of our salvation. In fact, hope in intellectual advancement is held in such high esteem that some people are willing to relinquish their autonomy to have its ideology enforced.

What are we really relinquishing? The answer: the solid ground of truth from our unwavering Creator. While progressives are looking to "new," the answer to our deepest needs will be found in the old.

A progressive mindset doesn't need or want an unseen being intervening in human history to guide them according to His purpose. Humanists believe their intellect will uncover the answers to all of life's conundrums. Humanity is the new sovereign. If you're not jumping on board with the newest thought trend, you are irrelevant and close-minded.

According to the Bible, however, there is nothing "new." (Eccles. 1:9). In other words, no amount of innovation brought about by human intellect will ultimately turn the tide in our fallen world. Don't get me wrong. We should continue to advance and reap the benefits therefrom. However, no matter how far we advance, we will still contend with the same underlying problems. The issues may recycle in new packaging, but they all stem from the same age-old source—sin.

Yet we mustn't throw our hands up in the air. The longer we elevate the human as sovereign, the more our culture will veer dangerously off course. And just because we may be secure in our faith doesn't mean that our children and grandchildren won't get swept up in the threatening current of this egocentric paradigm.

Is it too late? Now more than ever we need to turn back to God. Not because things are good or because things will be good if we do. We turn to God because things have been rough and—given our fallen world, our flesh, and the devil—they might continue to be rough until God drops the curtain on time as we know it.

Therefore, we turn to God because He provides the only true, living hope that the best is yet to come. But until His plan is fully realized, circumstances on Earth can get worse. Only God provides the buoy of faith to keep us afloat in the interim.

> "In a bewildering world of social change, political stalemate, economic decline, moral confusion, and disasters both natural (tsunamis) and man-made (nuclear reactor meltdowns), there is something firm to hold on to. There is light for the path ahead. There is a script, a story of God's saving work, in which we participate. This script orients us, indicates our location, bestows tasks and tools upon us, and assures us of our destination."[1]

So what now? If trials are what we can expect, then let us look back to look forward.

Thousands of years ago, God gave His people a lesson on how to perceive and respond to their trials. Ironically, the source from which I'm extracting such a lesson comes

---

[1] Elwell. Walter A., *Encountering Biblical Studies: Encountering the New Testament: A Historical and Theological Survey*, 3rd Edition (2019), 4, accessed January 15, 2020, https://app.wordsearchbible.com.

primarily from Exodus 20:20, offering us a nice pun for realigning our perspective on trials and tribulations.

With 20/20 vision, we can view our adversities for the purpose God intends for them to serve. The purpose is to compel us to concentrate on the author and perfecter of our faith in the midst of our trials, for He is our true source of hope in a tumultuous world.

It may be no coincidence that I wrote this simple study over three years ago; it had the same message then as it does today. I was pleased to be reminded of its relevance as we enter the 2020s.

This study is sweet and simple. Although Exodus 20:20 speaks for itself, I always find it helpful to have a guide through. Scripture does not reach its full potential until it can be applied to our personal lives so I pray this gentle nudge from God brings your past, present, and future trials into focus for God's glory.

CHAPTER TWO

My Life Was Normal Until...

Some of us can remember a time when life seemed pretty simple. Problems were either not recognized because we were too young, naïve, or sheltered; or someone else handled our problems to protect us as much as possible.

Others of us, however, cannot remember a time when there were no issues. Suffering has been a way of life as long as we can remember.

Most of us can agree that life is not fair. We made mistakes. Others made mistakes. We left others in the wake of our damage. We were the direct or collateral damage of others. Forces outside of anyone's control commandeered our life or the life of someone we love.

At the turn of the century, a lovely family of four set out for a fun holiday vacation at a seaside resort. Leading up to the trip, everything in this family's life was normal, even routine. The parents' professional life afforded them this time of relaxation with their two children.

Little did they know that the trip would change everything. While the parents shopped at the resort's stores, one of their children was abducted from the nearby hotel bed in which she napped. Despite the fact that one of the adults had been checking in on the kids every thirty minutes, their little girl was gone. And she has not been seen since.

The story is one of shock, anger, and heartbreak. Although here it is a fictional story, there are thousands like it that are playing out in the world every day. How can this happen to an innocent child and a loving family?

The truth is, life can change on a dime. In such times of terror what truth can we trust?

Let's examine the burgeoning nation of Israel to see how God instructed them as the growing pains from their divine purpose began to emerge. Little did they know that the world as they knew it was about to be turned upside down.

We meet the Israelites right after Joseph welcomed the families of the sons of Jacob into Egypt to escape the seven-year famine in the area.

Things were going well. Even after their earthly benefactor, Joseph, died "the people of Israel were fruitful and increased greatly; they multiplied and grew exceedingly strong, so that the land was filled with them" (Exodus 1:7). The descendants of Jacob had become an official people, race, and nation blessed by Yahweh.

Then, almost overnight, everything changed. "Now there arose a new king over Egypt, who did not know Joseph" (Ex. 1:9). This king decided to "deal shrewdly with them, lest they multiply, and, if war breaks out, they join our enemies and fight against us and escape from the land" (Exod. 1:10). For the next four hundred years, the Egyptians "made their lives bitter with hard service, in mortar and brick, and in all kinds of work in the field. In all their work they ruthlessly made them work as slaves" (Exod. 1:14). To make matters worse, Pharaoh commanded the Hebrew midwives to kill all Hebrew baby boys. "If it is a son, you shall kill him, but if it is a daughter, she shall live" (Exod. 1:16). Life was not fair.

This new Egyptian king did not study history. He had no idea that a Hebrew had saved his people. It would have behooved the king to acknowledge that he might not have even been born if not for the gracious intervention of a humble Hebrew and his faithful God. Now the new king was going to persecute the same people who saved him just because the sheer number of Israelites caused him alarm. What if they turned against him? He wasn't going to wait to find out.

Reflection/Study Questions

1. Read Exodus chapters 1 and 3.

   _____

   _____

   _____

   _____

2. What was the Israelites' standing in Egypt before the new king came into power there? (Exod. 1:5-7)?

   _____

   _____

   _____

   _____

3. What was the new king's approach to the Israelites? How did he devise this approach? For what reason did he do this? (Exod. 8-10)

_____

_____

_____

_____

4. How did the Egyptian king's plan work out? (Exod. 14:26-31)

_____

_____

_____

_____

_____

5. Have you ever schemed to overcome a perceived threat? Looking back, would it have been better to trust God? Why or why not?

6. What is the importance of remembering God's intervention in history, both for you personally and the world? (Exod. 1:8)

7. Has success ever "invited" persecution or hardship in your life? Explain.

_____

_____

_____

_____

8. How does the Bible tell us to respond to people who try to shut us down? (Matt. 5:44; Rom. 12:19)

_____

_____

_____

_____

Thanks to Joseph, who saved Egypt and the surrounding nations from famine, the Israelites enjoyed a good life in Egypt. God's providence saw to it that Joseph was exalted to second-in-command there. While in command, Joseph not only promoted the interests of his people, but those of the Egyptians as well. Sadly, Joseph's legacy was forgotten and with it the Hebrews' quality of life.

The new king saw how numerous the Israelites had become and felt threatened. He used his human intellect to devise a scheme to protect Egypt from the perceived threat of the Israelites. In the king's mind, it seemed logical to stop a threat before it materialized and stop it using all the means he had at his disposal.

Even though this new king of Egypt had the resources of the most powerful empire on the Earth at the time, his power and intellect paled in comparison to the one true God. And God proved it. God harnessed His supernatural power over the universe to see His plan through and protect His people. In the end, God allowed His people to escape Egypt by crossing the Red Sea on dry land while the Egyptian military muscle drowned in the looming waters.

The new Egyptian king would have been wise to remember how God always protects His people. History is important, especially biblical history. When we forget how God has intervened to bless and protect His people (including us!), we dilute the power of our faith. God's interventions strengthen our faith for future trials. When the going gets tough, the tough remember God's faithfulness to pull us through. History demonstrates (even to those who don't believe) how God is an active, guiding force in the world.

The Egyptian king opened the door to God's intervention through his shortsighted sin. He was threatened. Sometimes being at the top stirs up jealousy in others. Where jealousy exists, persecution usually follows. "For where jealousy and selfish ambition exist, there will be disorder and every vile practice" (James 3:16). Those who feel threatened by your presence may seek to sabotage your place in the organization, family, or community. But we who have faith in the Lord need not fear their schemes.

Joseph also had his share of hardships before he was exalted to second-in-command for God's good purpose. We would be prudent to heed his perspective. "As for you,

you meant evil against me, but God meant it for good, to bring it about that many people should be kept alive, as they are today" (Gen. 50:20). When someone persecutes us, we respond in love, keeping the faith. We wait patiently for God to intervene with justice because ultimately God has a purpose even for this trial, and it's a good one.

CHAPTER THREE

Through the Looking Glass

*J*ust when we think the tide has turned in our lives, people break their promises, expectations are dashed, and the journey continues. We trusted God with our trial, yet we see no immediate relief in sight.

Carol and Don were a lovely young couple who wanted to have a child but Carol struggled with infertility. Like most people in their situation, they turned to in vitro fertilization for a potential solution—hope for a way out of their predicament. And it worked. The procedure enabled God to bless them with a beautiful child.

Their hearts, however, longed for more. They trusted God with their plight and prayed for the miracle of natural conception. Sadly, nothing materialized.

As they endured the heart-rending road of infertility, they returned to the option of in vitro fertilization. Yet this time Carol lost embryo after embryo. So, they tried adoption. Still, nothing worked out. The emotional toil they experienced was excruciating. Years passed while they pursued their dream of having a child. Had God forgotten about His faithful servants?

With two embryos left and the passing time adding years to their life, they decided it was now or never. They would gird their faith and resilience for another trek down what had been for them a broken road.

On the eve of their last attempt with the final remaining embryo, Carol prayed anew that God's will be done. She imagined the embryo storage bank holding their last little baby and the Holy Spirit saying, "I didn't want to leave this one behind." Perhaps this was the one.

And it was. The last embryo became a viable pregnancy for a precious rainbow baby.

God's purpose had been to give every one of those embryos a chance at life. And Carol and Don will enjoy the presence of each of them in heaven for eternity. Had any one of the earlier implantations resulted in a viable pregnancy, the remaining embryos may not have been given that chance at life. But God had a better plan. And His plan took patience and perseverance and a great dose of faith to endure until His blessing materialized.

Similarly, the Israelites had had to endure disappointment. We left off our story as God sent Moses to free the Israelites from Egyptian bondage. God provided His people with a solution; a way out of their predicament. God also promised them a land of their own, flowing with milk and honey.

Like Carol and Don, however, they did not receive their blessing contemporaneously with their solution. Before they received their blessing, they had to wander through the desert for forty years.

From the Israelites' perspective, being freed from Egypt without immediately crossing the threshold into the Promised Land was too much to bear. They left the solution for their problem up to God, but found themselves wandering in the desert devoid of resources.

So they did what most of us would do when our circumstances pivot and our expectations are not fully met. The Israelites grumbled against the Lord. They tested the Lord. They cheated on the Lord. And in so doing, they opened themselves up to attack:

> "But the people thirsted there for water, and the people **grumbled** against Moses and said, "'Why did you bring us up out of Egypt, to kill us and our children and our livestock with thirst?'" (Exod. 17:3)

> "…they **tested** the Lord by saying, "is the Lord among us or not?" (Exod. 17:7)

> "Then Amalek came and **fought with** Israel at Rephidim." (Exod. 17:8).

In addition, the Israelites tried to exert control by making golden idols in which they could put their hope (Exod. 32:1).

The Israelites might have rationalized their attitude with the belief that God had broken His promise. What they didn't know was that God had a better plan to train them to appreciate and enjoy their future blessing even more. He needed them to have their "desert" experience in order to reveal the true posture of their hearts toward Him.

God didn't want spoiled children entering into His blessing, ones who would plunder the wealth and credit themselves. He wanted faithful servants who would be witnesses to the world of His goodness and sovereignty. But God was going to have to work humility and trust into them.

A lot of us as parents initially have to condition humility and trust into our little children as well. My two-year-old son and I recently flew back from visiting extended family. Before we boarded the plane we played in the waiting area. We raced up and down the hallway. Why? I needed to wear him down enough that he would almost collapse in my arms during the flight. He had so much energy; he had already almost run through security, up an elevator, and out the front door. Once he had expended most of his energy, he had to rely on me to lead him and care for him.

Perhaps similarly, God needed the Israelites to expend some physical and spiritual energy on the journey through the barren desert so they would to look to Him for care and protection instead of relying solely on themselves. Whether they could see it in the moment or not, God would not stop until they did. What a loving Father He is to wait until we collapse into His arms so He can care for us! He wants the best for His children.

Reflection/Study Questions

1. Read Exodus 16-17. Jot down your observations.

   _____

   _____

   _____

   _____

2. How did the Israelites perceive that Moses and/or God had failed them? Have people failed you? Does it seem like God has failed you? How and why should you shift your paradigm on this?

   _____

   _____

   _____

   _____

3. If God prescribes a way for something to be done, but it doesn't immediately work, do you take matters into your own hands? Why or why not?

4. How might your efforts equate to idol worship? (Col. 3:5)

5. Have you ever found yourself in a barren or desert season of life where you were in want rather than plenty (energy, health, friends, joy, peace, love, provision, necessities, faith, etc.)? Explain.

_____

_____

_____

_____

6. Honestly assess your attitude during that dry season. How did yours compare to the Israelites' attitude in the desert?

_____

_____

_____

_____

7. How did God provide for the Israelites' need despite their poor attitude? (Exod. 16)

___

___

___

___

8. Do you believe God would do the same for you today? Why or why not? (Matt. 7:11, Phil. 4:19, John 15:16)

___

___

___

___

Exodus 17 contains part of the account of the Israelites wandering in the desert after being liberated by God from horrible enslavement. One might assume they were skipping through the desert singing songs of praise on their way to the Promised Land. Right? Wrong.

As we read Exodus 17 we don't find them rejoicing at all. On their way to the Promised Land they had to cross a desert. The desert was no oasis. They focused on their circumstances and their surroundings: sand, sun, rocks. No water, food, or shade. And worse yet, no end in sight.

When we are faced with "desert" circumstances we generally respond the same way. We grumble against the Lord: "Why is this happening to me?" We test the Lord: "Does He love me or not?" "Can we believe His word or not?" We look to other solutions when we believe God does not hear our cries. Our human response leaves us thirsty, suffering, doubting, and open to attack by the enemy.

In the desert, the Israelites had no control over the most basic necessities of life. They had to rely on God. And He delivered. But that didn't stop them from grumbling and testing the Lord. The adversity of the desert revealed the true posture of their hearts.

The human heart is bent on control. Sometimes we will go to great lengths to make sure our will is done. This reveals a lack of trust in God. Jesus taught us to pray *"thy will* be done on earth as it is in heaven" (Matt. 6:10). Jesus had to submit to God's will in the Garden of Gethsemane when He asked that this cup pass from Him, but *"thy will be done"* (Luke 22:42).

Anything we trust more than God becomes an idol. When we seek something God has prohibited, we commit idolatry. "Put to death, therefore, what is earthly in you: sexual immorality, impurity, passion, evil desire, and covetousness, which is idolatry" (Col. 3:5). We must not allow our dependence on anything to grow to the point that it becomes an idol. We need not fall back on anything other than the Word of the Lord to guide our steps on the right path.

CHAPTER FOUR

Bringing the Desert into Focus

*L*ife is messy. How we deal with this foregone conclusion will affect the quality of our reality. If we want a life of transcendent joy, we need to align our perception of this inevitability with God's purpose.

Thankfully, God is pretty straightforward when it comes to His purpose for our trials. If we can glean from His vision, then we can bring our "desert" experiences into focus for a blessed life.

One of my family's favorite movies is *Willie Wonka and the Chocolate Factory*. In it, Charlie is a humble kid who endures the hardship of poverty. Providence gives him the lucky Golden Ticket to tour Willie Wonka's mysterious Chocolate Factory. Unbeknownst to Charlie and the other winners, Wonka is looking for a suitable heir and is particular on one point: that such an heir has good character. Through the interview process, every one of the contestants except Charlie is eliminated for exhibiting impatient, insolent, and spoiled behavior. These children didn't like or honor discipline, respect, or patience. In the words of the character Veruca Salt, they wanted what they wanted and they wanted it *now*!

As we saw in the last chapter, the Israelites did not like the desert. The journey was arduous. Everywhere they looked was more of the same: nothing. They couldn't solve their own problems; they were too exhausted and the desert offered no resources anyway. They wanted the Promised Land and they wanted it *now*!

As their leader, Moses sought God's wisdom. And true to form, God supernaturally enabled Moses to bring manna and quail from nothing. However, God's provision did not stop the Israelites from grumbling. The Israelites needed an attitude adjustment. And God obliged, starting in the desert and then moving to the mountaintop.

God knew He had to reset the Israelites' perception of their desert journey. In the midst of their complaining "Moses said to the people, "Do not fear, for God has come to **TEST** you, that the **FEAR** of Him may be before you, that you may **not sin**'" (Exod. 20:20, emphasis added).

God has at least two purposes for His tests. As Exodus 20:20 highlights, they are to 1) evoke in us a fear of the Lord and 2) keep us within God's bumper lanes for righteous living. In other words, God tests us to teach us that He, the holy God and Creator of the universe is in control and our response to this is most wisely exercised through obedience.

God doesn't want us to develop fair-weather faith, the kind that withers at the first sign of persecution. God wants strong faith that withstands the trials of this life. His tests not only train us for our purpose, but for the eternity to come. Tests refine and cultivate our faith to endure the tough stuff to get us from where we are to where we need to be.

> "In this you rejoice, though now for a little while, if necessary, you have been grieved by various trials, so that the tested genuineness of your faith—more precious than gold that perishes though it is tested by fire—may be found to result in praise and glory and honor at the revelation of Jesus Christ" (1 Pet. 1:6-7).

Fear may have an unhealthy connotation, culturally speaking. But when we fear the Lord we revere and respect His holiness. Fear of God keeps us in the bumper lanes of His Word. It keeps us from sinning.

Scripture teaches that fear of the Lord is the beginning of wisdom (Prov. 1:7, 9:10). Fear of God enables us to fall under His will, which is the safest place to be. The testing we experience through our desert experiences most effectively cultivates our character to receive the wisdom that comes from fearing God.

When you find yourself wandering in the proverbial desert; when you don't receive your blessings concurrently with your deliverance, when your journey takes a turn and then keeps on going with no end in sight, when you are tempted to take matters into your own hands to expedite artificial relief, God may be walking you through a test of your faith. Pass that test by turning to God's Word for the wise response.

Reflection/Study Questions

1. Read Exodus 19-20. Jot down your observations.

   _____

   _____

   _____

   _____

2. How did Moses explain God's purpose for the Israelites' desert experience? (Exod. 20:20, Deut. 8:2)

   _____

   _____

   _____

   _____

3. What is the purpose of God's testing? Are God's tests good for us? (James 1:2-4, Exod. 20:20, 1 Pet. 1:7, Zech. 13:9)

_____

_____

_____

_____

4. What is the purpose of fearing God? (Prov. 1:7, 4:6-7, 9:10, James 3:17)

_____

_____

_____

_____

5. Read Exodus 1:17. How did the midwives respond to the king's command to kill newborn boys? What was the reason provided in Scripture for why they responded the way they did?

_____

_____

_____

_____

6. Who benefitted from the midwives' fear of the Lord?

_____

_____

_____

_____

7. What is the benefit of obeying God? (Acts 5:32, John 9:31; 14:21, Josh. 1:8, Prov. 14:12, Rom. 5:12)

8. Do you find it easier to follow society's rules for living or God's? Why or why not?

God's 20/20 vision from Exodus 20:20 gives us a new perspective of our trials. It means viewing them through the looking glass of fear—a reverential fear of God.

Fearing God means we acknowledge His holiness and; therefore, obey God even when we are desperate. We trust Him with all our needs. We look to Him to equip us with tools to make it through tough times. We have confidence that we aren't alone.

What the Israelites really wanted was control. But God wanted to discipline them to submit to Him instead. The desert was the best place to force the issue. With no resources what choice did they have?

Moses taught the Israelites that God was simply using their experience to test their faith and train them to live in obedience to Him.

Rest assured, God never tempts us to sin. "Let no one say when he is tempted, '"I am being tempted by God,"' for God cannot be tempted with evil, and he himself tempts no one'" (James 1:13). God's tests have the opposite purpose. God's tests lead to life; Satan's temptations lead to death.

"Count it all joy, my brothers, when you meet trials of various kinds, for you know that the testing of your faith produces steadfastness. And let steadfastness have its full effect, that you may be perfect and complete, lacking in nothing" (James 1:2-4).

God's tests enable us to endure the trials of this life when they come. They cultivate and refine our faith so that we reflect the character of Jesus Christ rather than the desires of our fallen, sinful flesh. The result is to become a person perfect and complete who lacks nothing.

Most people would escape all desert experiences if they could. They would not patiently endure hardship for the benefits that the conditions produce in their character.

But by enduring with obedience, we open the doors to God's blessings. The midwives are the perfect example. "But the midwives feared God and did not do as the king of Egypt commanded them, but let the male children live" (Exod. 1:17). The midwives feared God more than they feared the Egyptian king. What was the result? "So God dealt well with the midwives. And the people multiplied and grew very strong" (Exod. 1:20).

All worldly wisdom would have cautioned the Hebrew midwives against disobeying the most powerful king in the land. Surely they were writing their own death sentences. But because their fear led them to obey, God ordained their circumstances to protect them. We too can receive His wisdom to live a blessed and abundant life of love, joy, and peace when we obey.

CHAPTER FIVE

Insight on the Mountaintop

As a young man, Brad wanted success. First on his list was a law degree. Check. Next, the highest-paying job in town. Check. He imagined the respect he could garner by adorning walls with his awards and wooing others with his money and influence.

The downside of his ambition was the astute awareness of the achievements of others against which he measured his own. There was always someone smarter, better, more successful than he. He tried upping his game, but forces seemed to be working against him. Instead of happiness and honor he experienced disappointment and humiliation.

Circumstances got so dire that Brad decided God didn't love him.

One day he noticed a Bible in the drawer of his nightstand. How did that get there? he wondered. Out of curiosity he reached for it. Without any effort, its pages fell open to a chapter he didn't recognize. The first words he read, "Vanity of vanities, says the Preacher, vanity of vanities! All is vanity" (Eccles. 1:2).

A lump rose in Brad's throat. Something about those words pierced his heart. *All* is vanity. Did God intend this to be a message for him? If so, what did it really mean?

It took a few more years of hard knocks but Brad finally got the message. His desire for worldly success, honor, and riches amounted to vanity, a worthless and fleeting vapor that added nothing fruitful to his life. The things he coveted did nothing to glorify God. His search for significance in the world caused him to miss the true purpose of his life, which God had designed for him.

Through the clarity of God's Word, Brad could see that the difficulty of God's testing actually led him to a more fulfilling life. The blessings of his life are now all the sweeter because he knows that God loved him so much that he took away what Brad *wanted* in order to give him what he *needed*. Brad couldn't have come to this realization without the wisdom that God shared with him through His holy Word.

God is not finished with us in the desert. Indeed, there are other places He may take us. In the case of the Israelites, this other place was the mountaintop. God's two-step plan to prepare the Israelites for their blessing also required an encounter with Him on the mountaintop. There He gave them the specific wisdom they needed so that a fear of Him was instilled in them and so that they would cease from sinning. God was leading them to the mountaintop, but they had to cross the desert to get there.

God is also leading us to the mountaintop, but we too will have to cross a desert to get there. The adversity we experience in the desert reveals and refines our character such that we now want to obey God.

The question is: *how*? The answer: seek wisdom. "The beginning of wisdom is this: Get wisdom, and whatever you get, get insight. Prize her highly and she will exalt you; she will honor you if you embrace her" (Prov. 4:7-8). Godly wisdom from a personal connection with Him on the mountaintop provides the knowledge to finish the journey and receive our blessing.

While on the mountaintop, all the sinning that the Israelites would be inclined to do in the flesh, God prescribed against in the Ten Commandments. Through Moses, God gave the Israelites His wisdom for how to obey Him. They could now apply God's understanding to their tests and extract insight and significance to enhance the sweetness for when they reach the Promised Land.

Reflection/Study Questions

1. Read Exodus 20:1-17. Summarize God's wisdom here:

   _____

   _____

   _____

   _____

2. How did the Ten Commandments guide the Israelites? Do these rules change when circumstances become more difficult?

   _____

   _____

   _____

3. What are the two commandments Jesus gives His followers? (Matt. 22:36-40). How do these commands connect to the Ten Commandments?

4. Are we saved by works? (Eph. 2:8-9)

5. If we are not saved by works, what is the purpose of seeking godly wisdom? (Eph. 2:10)

_____

_____

_____

_____

6. How do God's tests lead us to our purpose? (Exod. 20:20; 2 Cor. 1:4; Rom. 8:29; James 1:2-4)

_____

_____

_____

_____

_____

7. How can seeking godly wisdom help us shift our paradigm from trial to triumph, jeering to joy, and floundering to faith in the midst of our wilderness season? (James 1:5, Exod. 20:20)

_____

_____

_____

_____

8. How does God's wisdom add insight and significance to our tests and enjoyment to our blessings?

_____

_____

_____

_____

Fear of God convicts us to stop sinning and obey God. We approach God on the proverbial mountaintop to ask Him the questions: how do I live within your boundaries? How do I deny my flesh and the world? How do I resist temptation by the evil one? This is the process of seeking God's wisdom. The Bible says

> "My son, if you receive my words and treasure up my commandments with you, making your ear attentive to wisdom and inclining your heart to understanding; yes, if you call out for insight and raise your voice for understanding, if you seek it like silver and search for it as for hidden treasures, then you will understand the fear of the Lord and find the knowledge of God. For the Lord gives wisdom; from his mouth come knowledge and understanding" (Prov. 2:1-6).

How do we get His wisdom? Not on a literal mountaintop. We find God's wisdom in the unwavering truths of the Bible.

God has planned the rest of our story. Our purpose has His fingerprints all over it, adding significance to His tests. The lessons we garner from His tests propel us forward to our blessings with greater joy. They are the salt that adds flavor to our experiences. The mountaintop with God is where we receive the wisdom to convert our desert experiences into fruitful faith.

Just like the Israelites, if left to go the way that our hearts truly desire, we might unwisely fall into sin by worshipping idols and coveting material things, and by becoming adulterous, disrespectful, jealous, thieving, slanderous, profane, overly ambitious, and murderous.

Our culture tries to assure us that if it feels natural, it must be good. But God's wisdom tells us the opposite. Our natural tendencies lead us down the road to destruction. If we are not seeking God's wisdom, our natural default is sin.

> "Enter by the narrow gate. For the gate is wide and the way is easy that leads to destruction, and those who enter by it are many. For the gate is narrow and the way is hard that leads

to life, and those who find it are few" (Matt. 7:13-14).

We must intentionally focus on God's righteous and unchanging (trustworthy) rules for living in order to avoid that which comes most naturally to us.

Jesus sums up the Ten Commandments with these two commands: 1) love God with all your heart and with all your soul and with all your mind (Matt. 22:37) and 2) love your neighbor as yourself (Matt. 22:39). God calls us to live out His love for us by reciprocating it back to Him and to others. His law never changes, even through the ages and despite our circumstances.

It is important to remember that even though we desire to seek God and His wisdom in order to live a righteous life we are fully saved by grace through faith. Our obedience is a reflection of our salvation, not the means to our salvation.

It is God's wisdom that adds insight to our desert experiences so that we may partake of the blessings He has planned for us. "Know therefore that wisdom is sweet to your soul. If you find it, there is a future for you, and your hope will never be cut off" (Prov. 24:14). Our future is where we can live out our purpose to glorify Christ.

Thus, God's testing convinces us to fear God. Our reverential fear of God leads us to His wisdom. And God's wisdom helps us understand the purpose of His testing to enrich our blessings going forward.

CHAPTER SIX

Mountaintop Reconciliation

Shelby sat alone on Christmas morning. The presents she had for her sons lay unwrapped. Tears streamed down her cheeks as the ache in her heart swelled. After her divorce, and a lot of manipulation, her sons had decided to live with her ex-husband and his new wife.

Shelby's deepest pain stemmed from her husband's betrayal. Her sons wanted nothing to do with her because her ex-husband had convinced them that she had caused their divorce. Little did they know how hard she had fought to hang on, but she was no match for her younger doppelganger.

Now alone, she found herself stuck in an endless cycle of self-doubt and depression. On the prompting of her friends, Shelby began attending church, then a small group Bible study, then a support group.

God met her in her pain. She suddenly longed for a relationship her heavenly Father whose love she didn't have to earn. As the clouds began to part in her life, joy returned, even though her circumstances did not change.

Then one day, she received a call from her ex. By this point, Shelby had rekindled a relationship with her sons and through this grapevine, she learned that her ex's new marriage was on the rocks.

Shelby had learned to forgive her ex. She truly wanted what was best for all of them, so she expressed her concerns. To her great surprise, her ex-husband's brash nature turned quiet for the first time. Humbled, he expressed his appreciation. Then, he admitted he had done her wrong and asked for Shelby's forgiveness.

Shelby couldn't speak. Tears flowed, but this time they were tears of joy. She was already in a good place, but this act of contrition enabled her to soul to soar. Shelby experienced the blessing of reconciliation.

Perhaps our knee-jerk response to adversity is to question God. But God cares about our pain. It is real and He feels it too. Part of shifting our "desert" paradigm to see His purpose includes not repressing our pain.

God wants us to be whole, healed, and at peace. If we blame God, however, we are shutting out the source of peace and joy and love that will transcend every raw emotion that stems from our affliction.

Not everything bad that happens is a test from God. But terrible experiences can be used to strengthen our faith none-the-less. Take heart that God has overcome the world (John 16:33). There is more to God's story of your life.

Part of God's overarching goal is to get you from where to you are to where He has purposed you to be. And that journey requires not only testing, but also reconciliation—reconciliation between you and Him as well as between you and others. Part of the process of reconciliation is forgiveness—forgiveness between you and Him as well as between you and others.

God's purpose for the mountaintop meeting with Moses was more than a "faith reset." God was calling the Israelites to the mountaintop to reconcile with Him. Reconciliation heals relationships and the Israelites needed to do some healing with God.

While Moses was on the mountaintop the first time, the Israelites grew impatient and decided to craft golden calves in which they would put their hope. Such idolatry incensed the Lord who had just delivered them from evil. They essentially cheated on God, failed the test of patience, and further revealed their wayward hearts. Things had to be made right for God to open the doors to the Promised Land.

God's holiness is a burning presence. The Israelites did not accompany Moses to the mountaintop for this reason. Because of God's holiness, a meeting with God required a mediator. God chose Moses to serve as the Hebrew's mediator for reconciliation.

Even though Moses was a human not consecrated or made holy to God in order to see Him, God took the precautions necessary to protect Moses. Otherwise, Moses would have burned up, like any of us.

We too need to reconcile with God. Scripture says that we are at enmity with the Lord. "For the mind that is set on the flesh is hostile to God, for it does not submit to God's law; indeed it cannot" (Rom. 8:7). We have gone our own way, disobeyed, cheated on, and forsaken our heavenly Father. This hurts Him and us. We must reconcile to fully experience our blessings.

A huge chasm looms between God's holy character and our unholy character. The only bridge capable of spanning one side to the other is our mediator, Jesus Christ.

Jesus fulfilled the law given to Moses on the mountaintop. Jesus alone now serves as mediator with God. Through Jesus we receive forgiveness for our sins.

God is no longer waiting on a mountaintop to share the wisdom we need to atone for our sins. By accepting Jesus as our Lord and Savior we receive the Holy Spirit who continually convicts us to stay on the right course of godly living.

God did all the work for us. We can thank Him, therefore, for the experiences that got us to the point of seeking His wisdom in order to reconcile.

Jesus led a ministry of reconciliation. Just like Him, we are called to a ministry of reconciliation with others. Our lives and the world are full of discord. God looks to our lives to make sure we have reconciled with others to evidence and reflect His love in the world.

Whatever our life brings—however God may use those times to test our faith, we can be assured that good can arise from the ashes. Thankfully God wants to refine our faith and get us to look to Him in order to motivate us to reconciliation. Then we can lavish in the blessings of our Promised Land.

Reflection/Study Questions

1. Read Exodus 3:1-12. What surprised you?

   _____

   _____

   _____

   _____

2. Why did God command Moses to remove his sandals? (Exod. 3:5)

   _____

   _____

   _____

   _____

3. What emotion overwhelmed Moses? Why? (Exod. 3:6)

4. What is holiness and why does it matter that God is holy? (Isa. 6:3, 40:25; 57:15, 1 Sam. 2:2; Exod. 15:11)

5. Who is our mediator today? How do we access Him? (1 Tim. 2:5; Eph. 2:18; John 14)

_____

_____

_____

_____

6. How can abiding in Jesus change our life to reconcile with God and others? (Rom. 5:10, 11:15; Eph. 4:32; Col. 3:13; Matt. 5:23-24)

_____

_____

_____

_____

Moses had to remove his sandals because he was "on holy ground" (Exod. 3:5). Whatever purpose was served, the point is, God's holiness shines a spotlight on our unholiness.

> "For thus says the One who is high and lifted up, who inhabits eternity, whose name is Holy: 'I dwell in the high and holy place, and also with him who is of a contrite and lowly spirit, to revive the spirit of the lowly, and to revive the heart of the contrite'" (Isa. 57:15).

Such holy perfection brings forth a healthy, reverential fear of God. Moses felt it too. Moses' fear of God's holiness led to his obedience. His obedience led to blessings, not only for him, but for all the people God put under his care.

Fear of God does this for us too. When we fear God, we acknowledge His holiness. We do what He asks of us. Our obedience pays dividends in both our life and the lives of others under our care.

What we couldn't do alone, Jesus did for us. He died for our sins so that we may have access to the Father through

Him. "For there is one God, and there is one mediator between God and men, the man Christ Jesus" (1 Tim. 2:5). Those who accept Jesus are cloaked with His holiness. We have an express elevator through Jesus to meet with God personally on the proverbial mountaintop. Jesus enables us to be reconciled to God and receive godly wisdom directly from the Holy Spirit.

Our reconciliation with God changes everything. It casts out all fear of our circumstances. It aligns our purpose with His. "For if while we were enemies we were reconciled to God by the death of His Son, how much more, now that we are reconciled, shall we be saved by his life" (Rom. 5:10). Reconciliation with God leads to eternal life.

Once we reconcile with God, we want to reconcile with others. "Be kind to one another, tenderhearted, forgiving one another, as God in Christ forgave you" (Eph. 4:32). We are forgiven, therefore we forgive. But also, God requires us to forgive in order for Him to forgive us. Such grace evidences a contrite heart, which God purposes to cultivate in us.

We no longer have to climb to the top of a mountain to access God. Because of Jesus, we have the Holy Spirit abiding in our hearts. Thus, we can simply ask God for wisdom and He will give it generously to us through the Holy Spirit. "If any of you lacks wisdom, let him ask God, who gives generously to all without reproach, and it will be given him" (James 1:5). Once we have wisdom we know, and knowing is half the battle. Now go and sin no more.

CHAPTER SEVEN

Hope in the Desert

Our trials are really an opportunity for us to choose God's wisdom or our own. There's really no question about which one is the best answer. "But Jesus looked at them and said, '"With man this is impossible, but with God all things are possible'" (Matt. 19:26). Only God provides the absolute truth that gives us stable footing and a clear vision to endure any trial this life may bring.

Take Gideon, for example (Judg. 6). During a time in history when the Israelites chose to do what was right in their own eyes (Judg. 17:6), Gideon stood out from the rest. Not because of his grandeur, stature, power, or might. He had none of these. Gideon was the least of his clan. He stood out because he partnered with God in a time of trial and defeated a mighty enemy on behalf of the entire nation.

Gideon was the underdog. We all love to root for an underdog. Why? Because there's less hope that the underdog will prevail against the forces working against it. This was true for Gideon as well. He was weak, scared, and uncertain. The Israelites were being persecuted by the Midianites and they cried out to God for help (Judg. 6:6). If anyone specified their choice of hero, Gideon's name would not be on their short (or long) list. But God had other plans.

God called him "O mighty man of valor" and "Go in this might of yours" (Judg. 6:12, 14). What might? Not his—the Lord's. God fought His battle. Through God's strength and wisdom, little Gideon and his small army of shepherds and farmers defeated the intimidating enemy.

The point is, there's hope in the desert! Even in the tough season of life, God is going before us to fight our battles if we partner with Him. It may take some tough knocks and refining of our faith to get us to recognize our need to obey, but once we do, all things are possible, even with little old you and me. Remember there can be no

> Healing without sickness,
>
> Forgiveness without offense,
>
> Hope without despair,
>
> Second chances without failure,
>
> Finding without loss,
>
> Recovery without harm,
>
> Justice without crime,
>
> Redemption without sin, or
>
> Reconciliation without discord.

Thankfully nothing we experience in this life can separate us from the love of God. If we seek Him through our mediator, Jesus Christ, even if getting there requires us to trudge through the desert, we will emerge with faith enough to enter our Promised Land.

Wherever you find yourself today, there's hope. Seek God and His wisdom. Align yourself with His will as set forth in His Word. Patiently endure His tests while keeping a strong, unwavering faith. And you will be able to look back on your trials with 20/20 vision. God used those desert experiences to strengthen your character and your faith to prepare you for your most abundant blessings.

WORKSHEET 1

Your Desert Experience/s

Use this space to record your past and/or future experiences in the desert. Are you still there?

Did you grumble at the Lord? Explain. Did you test God? How do/did you believe He failed you? Did you cheat on God? What controls did you put in place to commandeer the situation? What was the result?

This is part of your story, and God will not waste any part of it. So write the details—your emotions: anger, disgust, doubt, sadness, despair, thirst and hunger for healing. Be honest, God already knows.

Looking back and taking the time to chronicle your experience in the desert is the first step to obtain clear, 20/20 vision for why God brought you there in the first place.

20/20 VISION

20/20 VISION

20/20 VISION

20/20 VISION

20/20 VISION

WORKSHEET 2

ENCOUNTERING GOD AND HIS WISDOM

Use this space to record your encounter with God in the desert. Did you make it to the mountaintop? Are you still en route?

If God has drawn you to the mountaintop, what wisdom did you glean from Him and His Word? How has His wisdom shifted your perspective of your desert?

If you have not made it to the mountaintop, be encouraged to reach for your Bible today. Read what it has to say. Glean from its wisdom.

Either way, pray for understanding. Today is your turning point. Record your prayer. Log the wisdom He has shown you every step of the journey through.

It is only with God's wisdom that we will achieve clarity—20/20 vision—for all that we endured or are enduring in the desert.

20/20 VISION

20/20 VISION

20/20 VISION

20/20 VISION

20/20 VISION

ABOUT THE AUTHOR

 SARA B. ANDERSON graduated with high honors from the University of Nebraska, Lincoln in Speech Communications. From there she earned her Juris Doctorate with honors from the University of Nebraska College of Law. Sara is now a mother of five children with her wonderful husband. She is also the founder and president of Fruits of Faith Ministries Inc., an online ministry, which endeavors to plant the word of God and harvest fruits of faith. Sara's great delight is unpacking the Word of God and defending its truths in a relative world. To that end, she is currently pursuing her Masters of Divinity with a cognate in Apologetics to combine her skills in logic and rhetoric with her passion for sharing the unchanging truths of Scripture.

www.ingramcontent.com/pod-product-compliance
Lightning Source LLC
Chambersburg PA
CBHW051409290426
44108CB00015B/2210